ISBN 978-1-332-27836-7
PIBN 10308124

This book is a reproduction of an important historical work. Forgotten Books uses state-of-the-art technology to digitally reconstruct the work, preserving the original format whilst repairing imperfections present in the aged copy. In rare cases, an imperfection in the original, such as a blemish or missing page, may be replicated in our edition. We do, however, repair the vast majority of imperfections successfully; any imperfections that remain are intentionally left to preserve the state of such historical works.

1 MONTH OF
FREE
READING

at

www.ForgottenBooks.com

By purchasing this book you are eligible for one month membership to ForgottenBooks.com, giving you unlimited access to our entire collection of over 700,000 titles via our web site and mobile apps.

To claim your free month visit: www.forgottenbooks.com/free308124

English
Français
Deutsche
Italiano
Español
Português

www.forgottenbooks.com

Mythology Photography **Fiction**
Fishing Christianity **Art** Cooking
Essays Buddhism Freemasonry
Medicine **Biology** Music **Ancient**
Egypt Evolution Carpentry Physics
Dance Geology **Mathematics** Fitness
Shakespeare **Folklore** Yoga Marketing
Confidence Immortality Biographies
Poetry **Psychology** Witchcraft
Electronics Chemistry History **Law**
Accounting **Philosophy** Anthropology
Alchemy Drama Quantum Mechanics
Atheism Sexual Health **Ancient History**
Entrepreneurship Languages Sport
Paleontology Needlework Islam
Metaphysics Investment Archaeology
Parenting Statistics Criminology
Motivational

STATE OF CALIFORNIA

The Resources Agency

Department of Water Resources

BULLETIN No. 117

RECREATION
AND
FISH AND WILDLIFE PROGRAM
FOR THE STATE WATER PROJECT

DECEMBER 1968

NORMAN B. LIVERMORE, JR.
Secretary for Resources
The Resources Agency

RONALD REAGAN
Governor
State of California

WILLIAM R. GIANELLI
Director
Department of Water Resources

STATE OF CALIFORNIA

The Resources Agency

Department of Water Resources

BULLETIN No. 117

RECREATION
AND
FISH AND WILDLIFE PROGRAM
FOR THE STATE WATER PROJECT

Copies of this bulletin may be obtained from:
State of California
Department of Water Resources
P.O. Box 388
Sacramento, California 95802

DECEMBER 1968

PUBLISHED BULLETINS OF THE 117 SERIES

No.	Title	Date
117-2	Del Valle Reservoir Recreation Development Plan	Dec. 1966
117-3	Lake Davis Recreation Development Plan	July 1965
117-4	Abbey Bridge Reservoir Water Resources Recreation Report	Dec. 1966
117-6	Water Resources Recreation Report: Oroville Reservoir, Thermalito Forebay, Thermalito Afterbay	Dec. 1966
117-7	San Luis Reservoir and Forebay Recreation Development Plan	May 1965
	Appendix C: Fish and Wildlife Development Plan	June 1966
117-18	Oroville Borrow Area: Water Resources Recreation Report	July 1968
117-19	Kettleman City Aquatic Recreation Area: Recreation Development Plan	Dec. 1966
117-20	Ingram Creek Aquatic Recreation Area: Recreation Development Plan	Dec. 1966

FOREWORD

Recreation and the enhancement of fish and wildlife resources are purposes of the State Water Project. They are established by State Law as activities and resources which are intended to benefit from the construction and operation of water development projects by the State of California.

The State Water Project will provide major benefits to recreation and fish and wildlife interests. In fact, major accomplishments have already been made, as the completed units of the project are now being used by recreationists.

Bulletin 117 describes the proposal for implementation of the program of the Department of Water Resources for including recreation and fish and wildlife enhancement features in the State Water Project. It gives the background of the statutory and administrative basis for the program, and describes the present situation as well as the Department's schedule for developing recreation and fish and wildlife plans over the next five years within the present framework of the Water Code.

The Senate Committee on Water Resources held a public hearing on this program in Lancaster, California on October 24, 1968. A draft of this Bulletin had been circulated to the Committee and interested agencies and groups prior to the hearing. The program described in the Bulletin is flexible, and may be modified by legislative or administrative direction, or to reflect funding or other conditions.

William R. Gianelli

William R. Gianelli, Director
Department of Water Resources
The Resources Agency
State of California
December, 1968

State of California
The Resources Agency
Department of Water Resources

Ronald Reagan, Governor
Norman B. Livermore, Jr., Secretary for Resources
William R. Gianelli, Director, Department of Water Resources
Robert G. Eiland, Assistant Director
Alfred R. Golze', Deputy Director
John R. Teerink, Deputy Director

Division of Resources Development

Wesley E. Steiner, Division Engineer
John M. Haley, Assistant Division Engineer

This report was prepared by

David E. Pelgen, Chief, Recreation Planning and Coordination

and

Floyd P. McFadin, Water Resources Engineering Associate

TABLE OF CONTENTS

		Page
I.	Introduction	1
II.	Davis-Dolwig Act	3
III.	Recreation Planning	5
IV.	Recreation Financing	7
V.	Recreation Task Force	9
VI.	Resources Agency Policy on Davis-Dolwig Act	11
VII.	Implementation of Resources Agency Policy	12
VIII.	Planning Program	16
IX.	Appendixes	
	A. Davis-Dolwig Act	19
	B. Resources Agency Policy Statement	27

Figures

1.	Recreation Land Use and Acquisition Plan (Preland)	4
2.	Recreation Development Plan (Postland)	6
3.	Recreation and Fish and Wildlife Costs	8

Tables

1.	Recreation, Fish and Wildlife Enhancement Planning Program, State Water Project	17

ABSTRACT

The Davis-Dolwig Act of 1961 provided that the development of new recreation sites, along with features that will enhance the State's fish and wildlife resources, be included as a part of the State Water Project. The Act also assigned responsibility for planning such features to the Department of Water Resources./ Financing is provided from State Water Project Funds, Tidelands Oil Revenues, and the State General Fund./ A number of recreation features have already been constructed at completed Project units./ Plans for the next five years are explained. Pertinent sections of the Davis-Dolwig Act are included as Appendix A. Appendix B outlines the policy of the Resources Agency for carrying out the Davis-Dolwig Program.

INTRODUCTION

Plans for recreation and the enhancement of fish and wildlife have been a part of the Department of Water Resources' planning for the State Water Project for a number of years.

The first expression of legislative policy to have a major bearing on the role of recreation and fish and wildlife enhancement in the State Water Project, appeared in the State Water Resources Act of 1945 (California Statutes 1945, Ch. 1514). A portion of that Act (as codified in Water Code Section 12581) states that:

> "In studying water resources development projects, full consideration shall be given to all beneficial uses of the State's water resources including ... preservation and development of fish and wildlife resources, and recreational facilities, but not excluding other beneficial uses of water ...."

The State Water Resources Act was the expression by the Legislature which initiated studies leading to the preparation of the California Water Plan. Thus, the Department has been under directive from the Legislature to give full consideration to recreation and to planning for fisheries and wildlife since it began work on the California Water Plan. Early in that work recreation planners and fish and game biologists were added to the planning teams.

More comprehensive instructions were given by the Legislature in 1958, when Section 345 was added to the Water Code and in 1959 when Sections 233, 346, and 1243 were added. As a result of these additions to the Code, recreation and fish and wildlife conservation were prominently included in the planning of the State Water Project.

The Burns-Porter Act was passed by the Legislature in 1959 and later ratified by the electorate in 1960. This legislation provided the authorization and financing for the State Water Project exclusive of onshore recreation facilities. The project includes among other things a system of reservoirs, aqueducts, and other facilities to develop and transport surplus waters of Northern California to areas of need primarily in the North and South San Francisco Bay areas and in San Joaquin Valley and Southern California. The system, now past the midpoint of construction, is being financed for the most part by General Obligation Bonds, Revenue Bonds, and moneys derived from tidelands oil sources.

The Burns-Porter Act named certain dams and reservoirs of the State Water Project which could include recreation features, and in certain cases, named in the Upper Feather River areas dams and reservoirs which had been planned solely for recreation and fish and wildlife enhancement purposes.

RECREATION PLANNING

The Department of Water Resources obtains the services of specialists from the Department of Fish and Game and the Department of Parks and Recreation in fulfilling its responsibilities under the Davis-Dolwig Act for planning recreation and fish and wildlife enhancement. Through annual interagency agreements with these two departments, fishery biologists, recreation planners, and other specialists work in Department of Water Resources offices with Department of Water Resources engineers. Because of this close working relationship, the plans are fully coordinated among the concerned department personnel, and the resultant recommendations recognize the interests of all of the potential water project purposes.

In addition to being coordinated within Department of Water Resources offices while under preparation, the plans are reviewed and approved in the Departments of Fish and Game and Parks and Recreation, and are returned to Water Resources as the recommendations of those agencies.

Following full coordination and review of the Department's recreation and fish and wildlife enhancement planning reports among cooperating state agencies, drafts of the reports are sent to other concerned state agencies and to concerned federal and local agencies for their review and comment.

The Department of Water Resources has for several reasons divided its recreation planning activities into two phases. The first of these is called Preland, simply because it is the work necessary before lands can be acquired. This work is financed by State Water Project funds, and in doing it the Department relies heavily on planning assistance obtained through contracts with the Departments of Parks and Recreation and Fish and Game. A report prepared under this Preland program is called a Recreation Land Use and Land Acquisition Plan and is quite general in nature. It shows the recreational uses proposed for all of the project lands, and shows any additional lands needed if the general project lands are not sufficient to accommodate the planned recreation activities. When the Recreation Land Use and Land Acquisition Plan is completed and approved, it becomes the basis for land acquisition if additional lands are required.

Figure 1 shows a schematic diagram of the steps in preparing such a plan.

Following the preparation of the Land Use and Acquisition Plan the process moves into the Postland phase -- the preparation of the actual detailed Recreation Development Plan.

-5-

This plan is based on the concepts of the Land Use and Acquisition Plan and depicts the kinds of development proposed and just where the facilities are to be placed. It contains projections of the numbers of recreationists that will use the project areas, and it contains estimates of the development and operation costs for the project. The preparation of the Recreation Development Plan, like the earlier planning, is a cooperative venture in which the services of specialists from the cooperating state departments provide assistance to the Department of Water Resources. Unlike the earlier plan, the preparation of this more detailed plan is financed from the General Fund.

Figure 2 shows a schematic diagram of the steps in the preparation of a Recreation Development Plan. The purpose of the Recreation Development Plan is to show to the Legislature the kinds of recreation development and fish and wildlife enhancement measures and facilities proposed, and to describe the benefits and costs that relate to them. Reports on these plans also provide the basis to recommend to the Legislature that funds to implement the plan be included in the budget.

The Department of Parks and Recreation uses the Recreation Development Plan as a basis for its design and preparation of plans and specifications for construction of the recreation facilities and assumes the responsibility for implementation of the actual recreation facilities. The Office of Architecture and Construction, Department of General Services, serves as the contracting agency for the construction of major recreation facilities for the Department of Parks and Recreation.

FIGURE 2

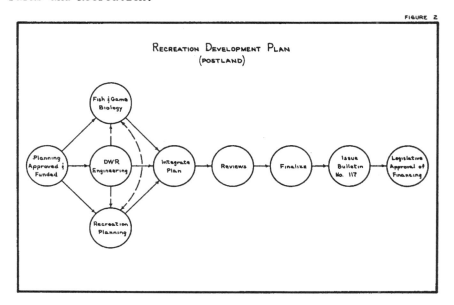

-6-

RECREATION FINANCING

The source of funds and the program developed for
financing the recreation and fish and wildlife elements of
the State Water Project are illustrated in a diagram shown
as Figure 3 entitled "State Water Project, Recreation and
Fish and Wildlife Costs". The diagram also shows the budgeting agency for each of the activities.

Water Code Section 11913 prescribes that funds
necessary for enhancement of fish and wildlife and for recreation shall be included in the budget of the Department of
Water Resources. However, in accordance with administrative
policy developed in 1965, the Department of Parks and Recreation actually budgets from the General Fund for recreation
facilities. The Department of Fish and Game budgets from the
General Fund for such facilities in areas under their jurisdiction, such as the Oroville Borrow Area.

The Legislature has declared that costs of recreation
and the enhancement of fish and wildlife should be nonreimbursable as distinguised from other water project purposes which
must be repaid by the water and power users. The Water Code
specifies that recovery of funds for these purposes shall not
be included in the prices, rates, and charges for water and
power. Water project funds used for recreation -- planning,
land acquisition, and the joint project costs allocated to
recreation -- are repaid to the extent available from tidelands oil revenues (Chapter 27, Statutes of 1966, First
Extraordinary Session).

Repayment from tidelands oil revenues for expenditures of water project funds for recreation or fish and wildlife enhancement is limited to $5 million per year. Because
of the magnitude of recreation expenditures and allocations,
the Department expects the full $5 million of reimbursements
to be required each year for the foreseeable future. Currently
there is a backlog of expenditures and allocations in excess
of the yearly limit. Thus, even though the Department's
expenditures for recreation are repaid in full and with interest, these expenditures can contribute to short-term financing
problems by depleting capital available at any given time.
This has been of concern to the Department in recent months
in connection with State Water Project financing considerations.

Another problem that the Department recognized in
the area of recreation and fish and wildlife financing is that
of meeting the costs of the onshore recreation facilities.
As pointed out earlier, design and construction of these
facilities and budgeting funds for them are responsibilities
of the Department of Parks and Recreation. As the planning

and land acquisition agency, the Department of Water Resources cannot help but be concerned about the difficulties in obtaining funds to complete the recreation facilities. As a matter of fact the Department in previous years has expended funds for land acquisition in anticipation of recreation facilities which now appear will not be provided. Some way must be found to insure that recreation plans can be implemented so that planning and land acquisition costs and expenditures can be justified.

The General Fund of the State is under heavy pressure by the demands of the great variety of activities and programs that are supported by it. Recreation programs are in serious competition with these other worthwhile and needed programs for limited dollars. To further compound the problem, recreation developments associated with the State Water Project must compete with a great many other State Park System projects -- parks, recreation areas, beaches -- for the limited funds available for the total Department of Parks and Recreation capital outlay program.

Financing the facilities and operations necessary for the mitigation of damages to fish and wildlife resources should be mentioned because it differs greatly from recreation and fish and wildlife enhancement. Requirements for preserving existing, or pre-project, fish and wildlife resources, or for mitigation of damages to them, produce no new benefits. These actions are much like relocation of utilities or replacement of features that the project would displace. Water project funds are used for fish and wildlife mitigation facilities and operations. These costs are project costs and are reimbursable.

One of the purposes of this report is to spell out procedures the Department of Water Resources intends to adopt in order to make the recreation and fish and wildlife portions of the State Water Project as meaningful as possible under the very severe limitation of funds available to it.

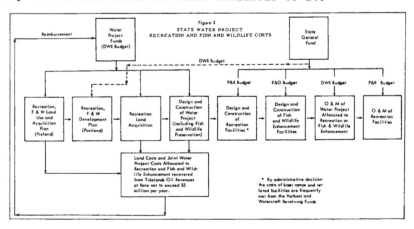

RECREATION TASK FORCE

In February of 1967, Mr. Norman B. Livermore, Jr., Secretary for the Resources Agency, appointed a Task Force to review the program for recreation and fish and wildlife enhancement for the State Water Project. This was done because it was recognized that the projected costs of the program appeared very high, and because the new administration wanted to review the policies of this important program and the requirements it was placing on the General Fund.

When it began its work, the Task Force recognized and identified 49 separate recreation or fish and wildlife features or projects. These included reservoirs, fishing access sites, aquatic recreation areas adjacent to aqueducts, fish hatcheries, ecological and wildlife habitat areas, streamflow maintenance projects, and others. Some of these were fully planned and described in official reports; some were on the drawing boards in various stages of completion; some had been only vaguely discussed and were little more than concepts.

From the planning data and cost estimates available, the Task Force identified total estimated capital costs for the program of $176.6 million over a 50-year period. These costs for the first ten years of the proposed projects amount to an estimated $105.3 million,or more than $10 million per year.

The Task Force reported its findings and recommendations in August 1967, in a report entitled "Report of the Recreation Task Force on the State Water Project". A number of recommendations were contained in the report. Some of them, such as those dealing with organization of recreation staff in the Department of Water Resources have been accomplished administratively. Some problems treated in the report resulted in action by others. Using information in the report, for example, the Senate Committee on Water Resources recommended assignment of the fishing access program to the Wildlife Conservation Board. Legislation to accomplish this was introduced and passed in the 1968 General Session.

The Task Force recommended that the planned program be scaled down by elimination of certain features planned for recreation that were not integral features of the State Water Project nor located on project land or water areas. It reasoned that features requiring additional or separated lands and new waters that would not normally exist in the project were not as clearly justifiable as projects at reservoirs or on the aqueducts that make direct use of the project. The

Task Force pointed out that the projects it suggested for deletion from the program could be built whether or not the State Water Project existed. Estimated costs of the projects recommended for deletion totaled $42.5 million.

RESOURCES AGENCY POLICY ON THE
DAVIS-DOLWIG ACT

The recommendations of the Recreation Task Force were reviewed by all of the agencies, organizations and groups that maintained an interest in the recreation and fish and wildlife program for the State Water Project. Some of the recommendations received negative comment by various groups. Not all of the critics, however, were in agreement as to the course of action that should be taken on the various aspects of the program.

In April of 1968 the Secretary for the Resources Agency issued a "Resources Agency Policy for the Davis-Dolwig Program" setting forth certain guidelines for proceeding further. The policy statement appears in Appendix B of this report.

The Secretary's policy statement assigned a priority system to recreation and fish and wildlife projects.identified by the Task Force for use in further planning and development. The priority system identifies several classes of reservoirs, fishing access sites, and miscellaneous projects. No projects were eliminated from further consideration.

IMPLEMENTATION OF THE
RESOURCES AGENCY POLICY

Since issuance by the Secretary for the Resources
Agency in April 1968 of his policy statement, the planning
program of the Department of Water Resources for recreation
and fish and wildlife enhancement has been revised. Additional detailed instructions are necessary, however, to provide for full implementation of the policy. Accordingly, the
guidelines set forth in this report have been prepared to
implement the Department's portion of the recreation and fish
and wildlife program for the State Water Project.

Implementation of the program consists essentially
of two parts: One is a continuation of activity already
underway, and the second part is an initiation of new activity to provide for an orderly procedure for these activities
not yet finalized -- both in furtherance of the Resources
Agency policy.

Reservoirs

Continuation of existing activity applies to the
first, second, and third categories. These are: (1) completed reservoirs, (2) reservoirs under construction, and
(3) reservoirs to be constructed. Work is underway to some
degree, or has been completed, at all reservoir sites in all
categories.

The preparation of land use and acquisition plan
reports (Preland program using project funds) will continue
to be processed in the four district offices of the Department. The Division of Right-of-Way Acquisition will monitor
the progress of these reports, and will proceed with the
acquisition of any additional lands needed once the Preland
report has received the approval of the Departments of Water
Resources and Finance.

Existing activity also includes reservoir recreation development plan reports (Postland program using General
Funds). These will continue to be prepared by the district
offices of the Department of Water Resources with assistance
from contract service personnel of the Departments of Parks
and Recreation and Fish and Game, with broad coordination as
at present. The recreation development plan is primarily
related to onshore facilities and operation matters, and is
based on the approved land use and acquisition report.

The impact of the recreation development plan on
the construction program of the Department should be discussed

in the report if there appear to be advantages in the Department including certain recreation construction in its program. Such construction of onshore recreation features and the time of construction of the basic water project requires advance financial arrangements with the Department of Parks and Recreation, and each will be handled on an individual basis as these situations occur.

Work on land use and acquisition plan reports around the various water project reservoirs, the acquisition of needed lands, and recreation development plan reports will be expedited to the maximum extent feasible, in keeping with the Resources Agency policy.

Fishing Access Sites

Fourth priority relates to provision of fishing access sites on the California Aqueduct which have been assigned to the Wildlife Conservation Board (Chapter 411, Statutes of 1968). The Wildlife Conservation Board is a very small agency and will need some help from the Department in getting this program started, particularly in making an early determination of land acquisition requirements. A formal report on land acquisition needs for fishing access sites is to be developed by the Board, and on approval of the plan by the Directors of Water Resources and Finance, the Division of Right-of-Way Acquisition will proceed with the acquisition of any additional land required in the same manner as under the land use and acquisition report for recreation at reservoirs.

See Water Code Section 11920 for additional guidance on the program for fishing access at aqueducts.

Miscellaneous Projects

The fifth and final category includes miscellaneous projects such as aquatic recreation areas, ecological areas, etc., each of which will be handled on its individual merits. Formal reports will be prepared for each of these for subsequent approval. In view of the fact that these projects are not fully integral with other physical features of the State Water Project, it is necessary to deviate somewhat from the procedures to be followed around the project reservoirs and along the project aqueducts. For the considerations set forth below, no additional land acquisition will be undertaken until there is reasonable assurance that funds will be available for construction of onshore facilities to complete the plan.

The Resources Agency policy statement lists four items* to be taken into account in considering the appropriateness of the several miscellaneous projects under the Davis-Dolwig Act. The items are largely self-explanatory, but for our purposes are amplified as follows:

1. The Resources Agency policy requires consideration of the <u>ability of local or other interests to construct and operate each facility or a substitute therefor in lieu of the State of California</u>.

In the Department's planning program the interest of local or other interests in construction or operation of each facility will be determined. Contacts will be made with boards of supervisors, local recreation departments or districts, and others. Consideration will be given to an expression of a state agency that it prefers to construct and/or operate the facility and can secure the necessary approvals and funds for implementation.

2. The policy requires consideration of the <u>feasibility of development as evidenced by completion and approval of definite planning reports as provided under established Davis-Dolwig procedures</u>.

The Department's reports on these projects will demonstrate a complete showing of economic justification before recommending a project for further consideration. Department reports on miscellaneous projects will be single reports entitled "Water Resources Recreation Reports" rather than dual reports as described; for example, in developing recreation plans around a reservoir. Under this plan land acquisition will not proceed until the entire plan is developed and approved and reasonable assurance obtained that funds can be secured to develop the plan.

3. The Resources Agency policy requires the <u>availability of State Water Project funds for land acquisition</u>.

This involves a sensitive policy determination which will be made by the Director of Water Resources following a determination of the approximate cost of such land and funding requirements of water-associated portions of the project.

4. The policy requires consideration of the <u>availability of general funds to complete onshore facilities</u>.

_____

*The underlined portions are quoted from the Resources Agency policy statement.

The Department would consider it inappropriate to expend water project funds for recreation lands only to see those lands remain undeveloped due to lack of funds for onshore recreation facilities. In order to avoid this, each report recommending a project for land acquisition and development will have a statement appended to it from the Directors of Parks and Recreation, Fish and Game, or Finance, as may be appropriate. This addition will state that timely appropriations to complete the developments recommended in the report will be given priority and included in that department's budget.

General Guidelines

Use of the five priority groupings in the Resources Agency policy statement does not imply that all of the actions on one priority must be completed before any work can proceed on the next lower priority. Planning and land acquisition on several projects of differing priorities might proceed at the same time; however, expenditure of manpower or funds on a low priority project would not be in keeping with the spirit of the Resources Agency policy if a higher priority project were delayed at the same time because of insufficient manpower or funds.

The listing of the projects within the individual priority categories in the Secretary's tabulation does not represent any order of preference.

With all categories of projects it will be necessary for the Department to maintain a continuity of coordination and exchange of information with other agencies working with us on these programs. This includes cooperating state agencies, the U. S. Forest Service, Federal Power Commission, and local interests such as counties, cities, and districts. Our water service contractors may also be involved. These relationships will be maintained primarily by the four districts of the Department at their level of activity.

PLANNING PROGRAM

Table 1, entitled "Recreation, Fish and Wildlife Enhancement Planning Program, State Water Project", has been prepared to set forth a proposed program for planning for recreation and fish and wildlife over the five-year period 1968-69 through 1972-73. The dollar amounts shown beyond the 1969-70 fiscal year are for budget planning purposes only at this time, and are subject to change. The table shows report progress and present and future planning effort for each of the recreation or fish and wildlife enhancement projects listed in the Secretary's April policy statement. An attempt has been made to schedule first those projects which appear to have an early need. It should not preclude a rearranging of program to the extent that it may be desirable to complete one facility in advance of another. The budgeted amounts for each year are broken down into project funds, used for planning prior to the definition of a land acquisition plan; and general funds, used for detailed recreation planning beyond the time that land needs are identified.

This five-year program reflects the priority assignments of the Resources Agency, the availability of funds, and the Department's estimate of time necessary to plan, fully coordinate and review with concerned agencies, and complete reports on the individual projects. If the opportunity develops to advance the planning for any of the proposals to a time earlier than shown on Table 1, the Department will advance the schedule for that work.

1   Indicates degree or completion or coordination with other agencies and preparation of reports

    I   Recommendations of Department of Fish and Game on land use and land acquisition received
    II   Recommendations of Department of Fish and Game on development received
    III Recommendations of Department of Parks and Recreation on land use and land acquisition received
    IV. Recommendations of Department of Parks and Recreation on development received.
    V   Department of Water Resources report on land use and land acquisition completed
    VI   Department of Water Resources report on development completed

2   Department of Water Resources planning work has been completed

3. Department of Water Resources planning work has been completed, but major revision in land acquisition makes that planning obsolete
    Additional recreation planning might be necessary

4   Not scheduled

5   Recreation planning included in project formulation studies and funded as part of that program.

6   Deferred in favor of Kern County's proposed Buena Vista Reservoir for which Davis-Grunsky financial assistance has been requested

7. Deferred in favor of more comprehensive proposal for acquisition and development by P&R through other than Davis-Dolwig Program.

8   Department of Water Resources planning has been completed and some of the lands have been acquired. Due to lack of current P&R
    interest, lands will be considered for disposal if not needed for fishing access program

9   Project funds

10 General funds

Appendix A

Davis-Dolwig Act

Davis-Dolwig Act
Article 1.   State Policy
(Article 1 added by Stats. 1961, Ch. 867)

11900.   The Legislature finds and declares it to be necessary for the general public health and welfare that preservation
of fish and wildlife be provided for in connection with the construction of state water projects.

The Legislature further finds and declares it to be
necessary for the general public health and welfare that facilities for the storage, conservation or regulation of water be constructed in a manner consistent with the full utilization of their
potential for the enhancement of fish and wildlife and to meet
recreational needs; and further finds and declares that the pro-
viding for the enhancement of fish and wildlife and for recreation
in connection with water storage, conservation, or regulation facilities benefits all of the people of California and that the project
construction costs attributable to such enhancement of fish and
wildlife and recreation features should be borne by them.

The Legislature further finds and declares it to be the
policy of this State that recreation and the enhancement of fish
and wildlife resources are among the purposes of state water
projects; that the acquisition of real property for such purposes
be planned and initiated concurrently with and as a part of the
land acquisition program for other purposes of state water projects; and that facilities for such purposes be ready and available for public use when each state water project having a potential for such uses is completed.
(Added by Stats. 1961, Ch. 867.)

11901.   It is the purpose of this chapter to provide
for the planning and construction of water storage, conservation,
and regulation facilities and associated fish and wildlife and
recreation features consistent with this declaration and to make
provision for funds therefor on a continuing basis, and to provide for the operation and maintenance of such fish and wildlife
and recreation features.

In enacting this chapter, however, it is not the intent
of the Legislature to diminish any existing powers of the Department of Water Resources, the Department of Parks and Recreation,
or the Department of Fish and Game, but rather to provide specif-
ically for the preservation and enhancement of fish and wildlife
resources and for a system of public recreation facilities at
state water projects as part of a coordinated plan for multipurpose
use of these projects.
(Added by Stats. 1961, Ch. 867; amended by Stats. 1965, Ch.93.)

Article 2. Definitions
(Article 2 added by Stats. 1961, Ch. 867)

11903. As used in this chapter, "project" means any
physical structure to provide for the conservation, storage,
regulation, transportation, or use of water, constructed by the
State itself or by the State in co-operation with the United
States.
(Added by Stats. 1961, Ch. 867.)

Article 3. Application
(Article 3 added by Stats. 1961, Ch. 867)

11905. The provision of this chapter shall apply to
the Central Valley Project and every other project constructed
by the State itself or by the State in co-operation with the
United States, including, but not limited to, the State Water
Resources Development System.
(Added by Stats. 1961, Ch. 867.)

Article 4. Planning and Construction of Projects
(Article 4 added by Stats. 1961, Ch. 867)

11910. There shall be incorporated in the planning and
construction of each project such features (including, but not
limited to, additional storage capacity) as the department, after
giving full consideration to any recommendations which may be made
by the Department of Fish and Game, the Department of Parks and
Recreation or any division thereof, including but not limited to,
the Division of Small Craft Harbors and the Division of Beaches
and Parks, any federal agency, and any local governmental agency
with jurisdiction over the area involved, determines necessary or
desirable for the preservation of fish and wildlife, and necessary
or desirable to permit, on a year-round basis, full utilization of
the project for the enhancement of fish and wildlife and for recreational purposes to the extent that such features are consistent with
other uses of the project, if any. It is the intent of the Legislature that there shall be full and close coordination of all planning for the preservation and enhancement of fish and wildlife and
for recreation in connection with state water projects by and
between the Department of Water Resources, the Department of Parks
and Recreation, the Department of Fish and Game, and all appropriate federal and local agencies.
(Added by Stats. 1961, Ch. 867; amended by Stats. 1965, Ch. 93.)

11910.5. Such recreational purposes include, but are
not limited to, those recreational pursuits generally associated
with the out-of-doors, such as camping, picnicking, fishing,
hunting, water contact sports, boating, and sightseeing, and the

associated facilities of campgrounds, picnic areas, water and
sanitary facilities, parking areas, view points, boat launching
ramps, and any others necessary to make project land and water
areas available for use by the public.
(Added by Stats. 1961, Ch. 867.)

11911. The planning for public recreation use and
fish and wildlife preservation and enhancement in connection
with state water projects shall be a part of the general project
formulation activities of the Department of Water Resources, in
consultation and co-operation with the departments and agencies
specified in Section 11910, through the advance planning stage,
including, but not limited to, the development of data on benefits and costs, recreation land use planning, and the acquisition
of land. In planning and constructing any project, the department
shall, to the extent possible, acquire all lands and locate and
construct, or cause to be constructed, the project and all works
and features incidental to its construction in such a manner as
to permit the use thereof for the preservation and enhancement
of fish and wildlife and for recreational purposes upon completion of the project.
(Added by Stats. 1961, Ch. 867.)

11912. The department, in fixing and establishing
prices, rates, and charges for water and power, shall include
as a reimbursable cost of any state water project an amount
sufficient to repay all costs incurred by the department, directly
or by contract with other agencies, for the preservation of fish
and wildlife and determined to be allocable to the costs of the
project works constructed for the development of such water and
power, or either. Costs incurred for the enhancement of fish
and wildlife or for the development of public recreation shall
not be included in the prices, rates, and charges for water and
power, and shall be nonreimbursable costs.

It shall be the duty of the department to report annually
to the Legislature the costs, if any, which the department has allocated to recreation and fish and wildlife enhancement for each
facility of any state water project. The department shall also
report to the Legislature any revisions which the department makes
in such allocations.

The department shall submit each such cost allocation
to the Department of Parks and Recreation and to the Department
of Fish and Game. The Department of Parks and Recreation and
the Department of Fish and Game shall file with the Department
of Water Resources their written comments with respect to each
such cost allocation, which written comments shall be included
in the report required by this section.

The allocations or revised allocations reported to the Legislature shall become effective for the purposes of Section 11915 upon approval by the Legislature.

It shall also be the duty of the department to report to the Legislature on any expenditure of funds for acquiring rights-of-way, easements and property pursuant to Section 346 for recreation development associated with such facilities. For the purposes of Section 11915 such expenditures shall become approved in the same manner as provided above with respect to cost allocations.
(Added by Stats. 1966, Ch. 27.)

Sec. 3. Section 11913 of said code is amended to read:
11913. The Legislature hereby declares its intent that, except as funds are provided pursuant to Section 11915, there shall be included in the budget for the department for the 1962-1963 fiscal year and each succeeding fiscal year and in the Budget Act for that fiscal year and each succeeding fiscal year, an appropriation from the General Fund of the funds necessary for enhancement of fish and wildlife and for recreation in connection with state water projects as provided in this chapter.
(Added by Stats. 1966, Ch. 27.)

11914. The department shall make any necessary revisions in the allocation of costs of any state water project works constructed for the development of water and power, or either, which would result from the expenditure of funds under this chapter for enhancement of fish and wildlife and recreation in connection with such works.
(Added by Stats. 1961, Ch. 867.)

Sec. 4. Section 11915 is added to said code, to read:
11915. All moneys deposited in the Central Valley Water Project Construction Fund pursuant to the provisions of Chapter 138, Statutes of 1964, First Extraordinary Session, and all accruals to such moneys so deposited, are hereby appropriated to the department for expenditure by the department without regard to fiscal years for the purposes of the construction fund, in amounts equal to allocations to recreation and fish and wildlife enhancement and to the costs of acquiring rights-of-way, easements and property for recreation development which have become effective pursuant to Section 11912.
(Added by Stats. 1966, Ch. 27.)

Sec. 5. Section 11915.1 is added to said code, to read:
11915.1. The provisions of this chapter shall not limit the department in the financing and construction of any of the facilities of the State Water Resources Development System pursuant to the provisions of Chapter 8 (commencing with Section 12930) of Part 6, nor shall they constitute a limitation on or modification of the responsibility of the department to make allocations of costs provided for in water supply contracts executed pursuant thereto.
(Added by Stats. 1966, Ch. 27.)

Sec. 6. Section 1.5 of this act shall not become operative if Senate Bill No. 2 of the 1966 First Extraordinary Session is enacted by the Legislature and becomes effective. (Added by Stats. 1966, Ch. 27.)

11915.5. For the purpose of furthering recreation in any project of the department, the department may exchange any real property it has acquired for property in the state owned by the United States which is of substantially equal value, whether or not such real property of the United States is adjacent to or needed for any project of the department. Such title or rights as the department deems necessary for the proper operation and maintenance of the water conservation, flood control or power features of any water project shall not be included in any exchange consummated under this section.

Any such exchange involving real property acquired by the department solely for recreation shall be concurred in by the Department of Parks and Recreation. Any such exchange involving property acquired by the department solely for fish and wildlife purposes shall be concurred in by the Department of Fish and Game. Any such exchange involving property acquired solely for fish, wildlife and recreational purposes shall be concurred in by the Department of Fish and Game and the Department of Parks and Recreation. Real property of the United States not necessary for a project of the department shall be acquired by the department by exchange under this section only if another agency of state government has agreed to acquire such real property from the department for the actual cost to the department of the real property which is to be given in exchange therefor; provided, that any amount appropriated to the department to reimburse it for prior expenditures for acquisition of such land shall be deducted from the actual cost. (Added by Stats. 1965, Ch. 1050.)

Article 5. Powers and Duties of the Department of Fish and Game and the Department of Natural Resources (Article 5 added by Stats. 1961, Ch. 867)

11917. The Department of Fish and Game shall manage fish and wildlife resources at state water projects, including any such additional resources as are created by such projects, in a manner compatible with the other uses of such projects. (Added by Stats. 1961, Ch. 867.)

11918. The Department of Parks and Recreation is authorized to design, construct, operate, and maintain public recreation facilities at state water projects. Before commencing the construction of any such facilities, the Department of Parks and Recreation shall submit its plans and designs to the local governmental agencies having jurisdiction over the area involved. The Department of Parks and Recreation shall make every effort to fulfill its responsibilities under this section by entering into contracts with the United States, local public agencies, or other entities, to the end that maximum development of the recreational potential of state water projects shall be realized. The Department of Parks and Recreation shall have the authority to establish and enforce standards for the development, operation, and maintenance of such public recreation areas.

The design, construction, operation, and maintenance of public recreation facilities at state water projects, and the management of project lands and water surfaces for recreational use, shall be subject to the approval of the Department of Water Resources to ensure that they shall not defeat or impair the orderly operation of any state water project for its other authorized purposes and the accomplishment of such purposes. (Added by Stats. 1961, Ch. 867; amended by Stats. 1965, Ch. 93.`

11919. Public recreation facilities in connection with state water projects are recreational areas. (Added by Stats. 1961, Ch. 867.)

11920. The Wildlife Conservation Board is authorized to design and construct public fishing access sites to aqueducts constructed as part of state water projects in accordance with such policies and procedures as may be established by the board.

To the extent practicable such fishing access sites shall be constructed upon lands acquired for state water project purposes; provided, that such additional lands as may be necessary for such fishing access sites shall be acquired by the Department of Water Resources pursuant to this chapter; and, provided further, that such facilities as may be necessary to assure the safe use of such fishing access sites by the public shall be constructed by the Department of Water Resources upon the appropriation of funds for such purposes by the Legislature.

Plans for such fishing access sites shall be subject to the approval of the Department of Water Resources to ensure that they shall not defeat or impair the orderly operation of any state water project for its other authorized purposes and the accomplishment of such purposes. (Added by Stats. 1968, Ch. 411.)

Article 6. Short Title
(Article 6 added by Stats. 1961, Ch. 867)

11925. This chapter shall be known and may be cited as the "Davis-Dolwig Act." (Added by Stats. 1961, Ch. 867.)

Appendix B

Resources Agency Policy for the
Davis-Dolwig Program

-27-

Memorandum

To : Honorable William R. Gianelli
Director
Department of Water Resources

Date : April 10, 1968

File No.:

Subject : Resources Agency
Policy - Davis-Dolwig
Act

From : Office of the Administrator

The attached statement of policy and tabulation of projects, which has evolved after our many detailed discussions, is transmitted for your information and implementation.

Please proceed with planning on the projects identified in the attached tabulation.

/s/ N. B. Livermore, Jr.
N. B. Livermore, Jr.

Attachments

The Resources Agency hereby adopts the following priorities and policies for development for recreation and fish and
wildlife enhancement facilities under the Davis-Dolwig program in
connection with the State Water Project:

Completed Reservoirs

First priority would include the development, on a
staged basis, of necessary facilities for recreation and fish and
wildlife enhancement at the major state water project reservoirs
that are already constructed. Department of Water Resources would
complete the acquisition of necessary lands with project funds.
The reservoirs involved include Oroville-Thermalito (including the
borrow area), Frenchman, Antelope, San Luis, Lake Davis and Los
Banos Creek, and Bethany Forebay. To the extent planning reports
for land acquisition and development have not been completed, they
will be expedited.

Reservoirs Under Construction

Second priority would include development of necessary
facilities for recreation and fish and wildlife enhancement at
project reservoirs now under construction; namely, Castaic, Clifton
Court Forebay and Del Valle Reservoirs. DWR would complete necessary land acquisition with project funds. Planning reports at these
sites would be revised at the earliest possible date to the extent
necessary by the Department of Water Resources in cooperation with
the Departments of Fish and Game, and Parks and Recreation.

Reservoirs to be Constructed

Third priority would include necessary facilities for
recreation and fish and wildlife enhancement at reservoirs to be
constructed, including Cedar Springs, Pyramid, Perris, Abbey Bridge,
and Dixie Refuge. Again, DWR would complete necessary land acquisition with project funds. Planning reports by the Department of
Water Resources, prepared in cooperation with Fish and Game, and
Parks and Recreation would be expedited.

Fishing Access

Fourth priority consists of fishing access sites along the California Aqueduct from the Delta to Cedar Springs Dam in San Bernardino County. This program is being taken over by the Wildlife Conservation Board. Department of Water Resources will work with the Board immediately to develop as many sites as possible as fast as possible throughout the entire aqueduct. An effort here should be made to construct as many fishing access sites as are feasible. To the extent additional land is required for this purpose, the Department of Water Resources should proceed to make such acquisitions with project funds. Access sites should be located on existing easements whenever possible and should not interfere with primary water supply purposes. Access sites should not be developed in the absence of a demonstration that a fishery will be present. Moneys from the General Fund will not be required for development of the fishery access program.

Miscellaneous Projects

The remaining 16 miscellaneous fish and wildlife and recreation projects set forth in the Recreation Task Force Report on the State Water Project include aquatic recreation areas, wildlife habitat, and ecological areas, fish hatcheries and other features.

Each of these projects will be considered on an individual basis taking into account items such as (1) ability of local or other interests to construct and operate each facility or a substitute therefor in lieu of the State of California, (2) feasibility of development as evidenced by completion and approval of definite planning reports as provided under established Davis-Dolwig procedures, (3) availability of State Water Project funds for land acquisition, (4) availability of general funds to complete onshore facilities.

PROJECTS FOR DAVIS-DOLWIG PROGRAM

Completed Reservoirs

1. Frenchman
2. Antelope
3. Lake Davis
4. Los Banos
5. San Luis Reservoir and Forebay
6. Thermalito Forebay and Afterbay
7. Oroville Reservoir and Borrow Area
8. Bethany Forebay

Reservoirs Under Construction

1. Del Valle Reservoir
2. Castaic Reservoir
3. Clifton Court Forebay

Reservoirs to be Constructed

1. Perris Reservoir
2. Lake Silverwood
3. Pyramid Reservoir
4. Abbey Bridge Reservoir
5. Dixie Refuge Reservoir

Fishing Access Sites

As planned and developed by Wildlife Conservation
Board but not limited to those set forth in the Task
Force Report.

Miscellaneous Projects

1. Peripheral Canal Recreation Areas
2. Ingram Creek Aquatic Recreation Area
3. Adams Canalside Habitat Area
4. Cadillac Canalside Habitat Area
5. Kettleman City Aquatic Recreation Area
6. Tupman Aquatic Recreation Area
7. Buena Vista Aquatic Recreation Area
8. Peace Valley Aquatic Recreation Area
9. Frenchmans Flat - Piru Creek Fish Enhancement
10. Ritter Canyon Aquatic Recreation Area
11. Ritter Ridge Ecological Area
12. Little Rock Reservoir Fishery Enhancement
13. Oro Grande Wash Fishing Access and A.R.A.
14. Hesperia Trout Fish Hatchery
15. Mojave Mesa Aquatic Recreation Area
16. Warm Water Hatchery at Mecca

CPSIA information can be obtained
at www.ICGtesting.com
Printed in the USA
BVHW040917211218
536170BV00015B/531/P